The Book of Answers from your Birth Mother

A guided journal for Birth Mothers to tell their life story in their own words.

Dear Birth Mothers,

This guided journal is intended to give you an opportunity to tell your own life story, in your voice to your biological child. There are many questions in this journal, some light, some heavy. There are no wrong answers. Answer what you can and as honestly as you can, as if you were speaking directly to your child. Don't worry about grammar or spelling, what and how you write is uniquely you and an expression of your style. Your child will not judge you!

There is a section at the end of the book to include any pictures or mementos you would like to pass on as part of your legacy. Please attach any additional pages or consider creating a scrap book / life book to give the adoptive family to share with your child when the time is appropriate.

The more a child understands where he / she came from the stronger sense of self they will have. The more connection they feel to you and your family the more they will understand their adoption was a gift of love and selflessness.

As an adoptive mother, I want to thank you for completing this journal and gifting it to your child's adoptive family. The answers you provide could help create a sense of belonging and completeness for your child. Your child will read your stories and know them as truth regardless of anything they may hear from anyone else. You have a powerful voice which can heal misunderstandings and confusion. Please use this journal as vehicle to create clarity and express your inner self.

Giving life is the most beautiful gift any woman can give. You have my utmost respect and admiration for your strength and generosity! You are a true hero and nothing short of an angel!

Thank you,

Ms. Jenny Lynn
PO Box 4811
Mission Viejo, CA 92690

ms.jennylynn@cox.net

About the Author:

Author Ms. Jenny Lynn was raised with conservative traditional family values, with parents who happily participated in traditional roles. It wasn't until later in life she realized her clearly defined traditional sense of family was dysfunctional and holding her back from the unconditional love and commitment she believed family should provide. The preverbal white picket fence she spent years building was not working as Norman Rockwell led her to believe it would or should.

At a mid life age, Ms. Jenny Lynn decided it was time to create a life she had always dreamt of with a family true to her values. Without the support of her family, she divorced her husband of 10 years and filed the paperwork required to start the adoption process, domestically, internationally and through the foster care system, with the intent of being a single parent.

A few years into the process, the call that changed her life was received. "A birth mother wants to meet you and discuss possibly adopting her baby." From that first nerve wracking meeting with the birth mother and her family, things would forever be changed. A new oddly wonderful family unit was being nursed between herself and the birth family. Uncertain if an open adoption was the best theology of adoption for her, she moved forward with the agreement to foster a relationship between the birth mother and her son. What developed over time through all the fears and uncertainly was a love for her son's birth family rich in appreciation and gratitude. Never would she have guessed this would be the unconditional love and family commitment she had been yearning to find.

As the years have gone by, the visits with the birth family aren't as frequent as they were in the first year but the connection to them is still strong. Life's paths have taken different directions but like a true family, they can reunite at any occasion and pick up where things were last left without skipping a beat. They share in the milestone joys and frustrations which surrounds a toddler.

Today, Ms. Jenny Lynn's life is rich with unlikely family members who have come together for the love of her child. A special acknowledgment is noted to her fiancé Roger who encouraged her to do what is true to her heart and reminded her, as she cried many nights on his shoulder, she has the strength and ability to make anything happen! His incredible capacity to love those in rather different circumstances had opened her mind and her heart to new experiences.

"The Book of Answers" series was inspired by Ms. Jenny Lynn's son's God Mother, Sarah whom she considers more of a sister then a friend. Sarah, an adopted child sought out her biological mother at the age of 38. The questions she had and journey she traveled to find herself in a room of people who shared her same simile were nothing short of moving. With anticipation of Ms. Jenny Lynn's adopted son inevitable need to know answers to questions about who he is and where he biologically came from, "The Book of

Answers" series was created. Ms. Jenny Lynn thought "how ideal to hear his birth mother's written voice telling her views and opinions about her own life story."

This journal is one vehicle to be used to become familiar with the birth family regardless of their accessibility. It is an opportunity to tell the birth mother's family story from her point of view without interruption, in a safe non-accusing environment. An open adoption allows for this free exchange of information and can be a healthy way for an adopted child to understand it was through the love of family, regardless of circumstance, that brought everyone together to share their lives.

After all, we are all simply a branch of someone's family tree.

Dedicated To All The Angels On Earth:

I dedicate this journal to all the selfless birth mothers who have courageously chosen life over other options available to them. It is a true hero that puts another life ahead of their own. I personally believe the gift you are giving both your child and a waiting parent is one that will create grace and peace in your life. You are nothing short of an angel to both your child and the adoptive parent!

I hope, in exchange, your child's adoptive parent will be your angel, giving you piece of mind and confidence they will love your child as the awaited blessing they have been praying to receive. All adoptive parents I have known have had a genuine calling to nourish a family regardless of the stereo types associated with being single, married, divorced, gay or straight. It is a beautiful world we live in knowing the ability to love a child isn't bound to societal definitions of who we are as people. I have realized through my own experience, adoptive parents share the same concerns with birth parents: they are concerned they will be judged for their life circumstances. In reality no one is perfect, no one has perfect circumstances and no one willing to unconditionally love a child should be judged superficially for what is true to their heart.

While emotions run wild during an open adoption process, find faith in the belief that the child comes first. If birth parents and adoptive parents can agree to put the child's best interest ahead of all else, then the right outcome will prevail. It is important to me, for my son to know the respect I have for his birth mother. I want him to grow up knowing he has two mothers that love him enough to do what is best for him. I will teach him to honor her for giving him life and the opportunity for us to be family. He will know adoption is the ultimate expression of love a birth mother could give her child. I hope to teach him to recognize the soul and beauty in a person's heart by their actions, not their circumstances.

I want to personally thank my son's birth mother, Erin, for being the single most incredible person whom I have had the pleasure of knowing. While we come from very different worlds, I find we are just alike as we are different. I am in awe of her strength and determination to do what is right, regardless of her challenges. I sincerely hope she will always choose to participate in my son's milestones but understand whole heartily that she may want or need to disassociate with us in order to move forward in her life. As I would appreciate her being there for my son's seasons to change I will be there for hers. She is the one other woman in this world who loves my son every bit as much as I do. By knowing her and her family, I see my son in a more complete light. She truly is my angel. I will always regard her as such, no matter what challenges she faces or what path her choices lead her to travel.

More often then not, openness to a birth mother's continued involvement confuses people who have not been exposed to the open adoption process. They underestimate the bonding of the mothers. They assume birth mothers would be territorial over the child rather then appreciative of the opportunity given to the child. Throughout my adoption journey, I learned the kindest and most supportive people can come out from the most unexpected places. I found some heart breaking challenges with folks I'd assumed would be supportive with equally surprising love and support from folks I'd honestly didn't think would care. Neighbors, colleagues, social workers, attorneys, some times even strangers would encourage me in my hour of doubt and fear. I urge anyone going through the process to embrace the support from wherever it may come. Sometimes a person more removed from the situation has a clearer view of the bigger picture. Your biggest support may not come from your well intentioned, immediate family who may find comfort in the status quo or tradition.

One person whom has proven time and time again to be one of my angels on earth and has gone over and beyond the supportive role is my darling, Roger. While at first, Roger expressed his concerns and hesitation to assume the responsibility of dating a single mother with an infant child. He has now grown with me in loving my son as his own.

He could have bowed out gracefully, but he didn't. He chose to stay with "us" during the birth mother's pregnancy, the drama of the adoption process, the invasion of personal space inflicted by social workers inspecting our home and our personal lives, to the final court date officially declaring my son as my forever family. Roger could have taken the easy way out, but he stayed. Roger not only assumed but he carried my "baggage" I brought into our relationship. He gave me strength and comfort in times only he knew I needed it. He held me as I cried tears of joy and tears of fear on his shoulder. He convinced me to do what is right by following what is in my heart. He taught me to embrace the circumstances that brought my son's birth mother to me. He showed me the traditional way is only one possible way to create a family. Roger and his liberal ways stayed and enriched my life beyond description. Thank God! Roger has been and will always be my rock, the foundation in which my son and I can now build our lives upon. There is a saying: "With great risk comes great reward." I am so thankful he took the risk in taking this journey with me. The reward of being a family is truly great, especially when it can be shared with someone you consider your best friend!

One day my son will ask about his biological parents. I can whole heartily tell him about his loving biological mother, her bravery and her heroic strength. Hopefully he will already know her from a life time of birthdays, holidays and visits. When I explain we do not know who his biological father is, I'll have the opportunity to explain he needs to look no further then Roger's eyes to understand and feel his father's love.

Another angel and tremendous inspiration in my journey was my "soul sister" Sarah. I have never met a person who is so much like me in so many ways and circumstances. She truly is a non biological, spiritual sister to me. I'm fortune to have her in my life as a sounding board, advisor, mentor and often a mirror. Sarah's prayers and support have seen me through some very difficult times. I can always count on her for words of wisdom and insight, not to mention an often needed good laugh!

Sarah was the first to volunteer to write my letter of recommendation and guardianship letter to the social agency to satisfy one of the adoption requirements. While others hesitated and weighted in their liability for helping me out, she jumped in with both feet waving her pom poms and cheering me on all the way!

Whenever I would struggle with "Why can't I be like everyone else, happily married and having children in the traditional since?" she reminded me, I am nothing like anyone else. I am special to God's plan and God isn't required to explain his plan to us, but we are required to trust he knows best. We just need to do his work with whatever tools he gives us, even if that means a broken marriage and failed goals. She'd remind me there is always a higher power. She helped me to realize I had to experience those life challenges in preparation to answer my calling to be my son's Momma!

Sarah is now my son's God Mother and was a true inspiration for creating this journal. She sought out her birth mother at age 38. Her journey to find herself in a room of people, who share her same smile, moved me to create this journal as a vehicle of communication that is non-interrupted, nonjudgmental and all encompassing. Sure Sarah had an idea about her family health history as many adoptive parents are privileged to this information but what about the other less life effecting questions? Are my biological parents athletic, artistic, outgoing, introverted? What childhood experiences did they have? What were their relations with my biological grandparents? Can they sing or dance? So many natural curiosities.

It is my intention in creating this journal to lessen the gap in an adoptive child experiences between the love they feel for their adoptive family and their curiosity about their biological family. Through communication resolution can be found. If this journal helps just one child feel more complete or connected, then I helped to heal and enrich a blessing's life. If this journal helps just one birth mother feel her voice is being heard, then I have reinforced an angel's loving deed. If this journal helps just one adoptive mother feel she has support from the birth mother, then I have hopefully showed her how angels touch our lives and shower us with unexpected blessings.

Angels surround us everyday. Be open to experiencing them, as they often may appear very different from ourselves and may be assumed the least likely to change our lives forever! Once you realize you too are someone's angel, it will be easier for you to experience the blessings you receive and to notice the ones you freely give. Appreciate your angels. They were placed in your life by a higher power, for a reason.

This journal has been completed for:

_____

This journal has been completed by:

_____

The Book of Answers

A guided journal for birth mothers to tell their life story in their own words.

The Family Basics:
"The story of a mother's heart is a child's textbook"

What is your name?
When and where were you born and in what year?

Who comprises your family? Parents? Brothers Sisters? Aunts? Uncles? Cousins?

Have you or a family member ever been in the military? If so what branch? What years?

Do I have siblings? If so who are they? Are they full, half or non biological siblings?

Where did you grow up?

What are some of the common family traits?

Where did you go to school?

Are you or the family religious? If so what religion?

Do you work? If so doing what?

Do you have allergies? If so to what?

Is there any family medical issues I may have inherited?

What is your happiest memory growing up?

What is your saddest memory growing up?

If you could change anything about your childhood what would it be?

What family traditions do you enjoy?

Share a fond memory of your family:

Growing up, how did you spend your Sundays?

Describe your parents: Where they strict? Traditional? Absent?

Do you get along with your family? If not why?

Maybe We Are Just Alike:
"To know each other is to love each other"

What makes you laugh?

What makes you cry?

What is your favorite book or movie?

What is your favorite pet? Why?

What sports do you like? Did you play any sports? If so which ones?

Did you like school?

What subjects did you do the best in studying?

What food do you love and what food do you hate?

Do you prefer to spend time indoors or outdoors? Doing what?

What is your favorite color? Why?

Is your personality more outgoing and social or introverted and shy?

What is your favorite pastime? Why?

Do you prefer to hang out with a lot of friends or just a few?

Would you rather go out or stay in on a Saturday night? What would you be doing?

What do you do for fun?

Are you a "neat freak" person or a "comfortably" messy person?

Describe your personality.

Are you the center of attention or more of a spectator?

What is your favorite season of the year and why?

Do you enjoy practical jokes? If so what are your favorite ones pulled on you or that you pulled off?

Do you like to exercise or prefer not to sweat?

Do you enjoy team sports or one on one sports?

Are you handy with tools or better off to call a handyman? Explain:

Do you have a favorite college or professional team? How often do you watch them play?

What TV shows do you enjoy?

What if any musical instruments do you play? Did you ever take music lessons? Where do you play? How long have you been playing?

Do you consider yourself a singer? Are you a good singer or do your friends boo you off the stage?

Do you enjoy camping? If so where?

Are you a good swimmer? Did you ever compete or are you better suited to lounge in the pool on a raft?

Are you an optimist or pessimist?

What kind of grades did you earn?

Was studying hard or easy for you?

What extra curricular actives did you participate in high school?

What kind of movies do you enjoy?

Which board or card games do you enjoy? Are you a good winner or sore looser?

Your Unique and Personal Experiences and Opinions:

"I knew you before you were born and I want you to know me"

What is your most proud achievement?

In what ways are you sentimental?

What did you want to be when growing up?

As a child, did you play pretend? If so what did you pretend?

Describe your ideal vacation?

What was the best vacation you have been on? Why was it so great?

What would your friends say about you if asked? Would they be right?

What would your family say about you if asked? Would they be right?

What is your favorite part about the way you look? If you could change one thing about the way you look what would it be?

How do you like to celebrate your birthday?

What is your favorite holiday? How do you like to spend celebrating it?

Did you move around a lot or have you found the place you would like to live?

Where do you like to travel? Is there anywhere you want to go but haven't?

What kind of music do you enjoy? What is your favorite song, band or album?

Do you have any nicknames? How did you get the nickname?

What was the first election you voted for the President? Who did you vote for?

Who has been the moist influential person in your life? How have they influenced you?

Who do you most respect and why?

Who is your favorite actor / actress and why?

Tell me about the pets you have or had:

What have been your most favorite and least favorite jobs? Why?

What is your favorite charity? How do you support it?

Do you live a healthy lifestyle? If so how? If not, in what ways are you unhealthy?

What struggles have you had in your life?

What are you biggest success in your life?

What do you hope to achieve that you haven't yet?

Was an injustice ever done to you? If so what and how did it affect your life?

What scares you?

Do you make and or keep any New Years resolutions? What were they?

Are you happy? If not what steps are you taking to make yourself happy?

If you could ask one question from God what would it be?

What does God mean to you?

Do you believe in angels? Do you believe in miracles?

Have you ever been touched by an angel? What happened?

Do you believe in the after life?

What is the most memorable experience you've had?

What can the youth learn from their elders?

Who is the wisest person you ever met? What made them wise?

Is there anyone you feel you need to make peace with? Who and Why?

What is the most important gift we can give another person?

What do you feel your purpose in life has been?

What is the hardest lesson you've ever learned?

What concerns you most about our nation's future?

From whom have you learned the most in life? What have you learned?

Are there any misconceptions people may have about you?

What is the most important thing you want people to know about you?

Are there any personal or family secrets you want to share?

What is the first thing you typically think about each morning?

What is the last thing you think about each night?

If you pray, how often? What do you pray about?

What is the best gift ever received? For what occasion? What made it special?

Are you a good driver? How many accidents have you had? Where they your fault? How many driving tickets have you had? Did you pay the ticket or fight it?

Do you have any superstitions?

What is the best advice you have ever received?

What is your most develop talent? How do you use it?

What makes you homesick?

Who is your hero and why? Has it changed since your childhood?

What national news worthy event has most effected you? (911, Presidential Election, Natural Disaster?) How were you effected?

If you could spend one day with anyone in the world, doing anything you want, who would it me? How would you choose to spend your time with them?

What is the best concert you have attended? Why? Who was with you?

Do you have any advise on how to be wise with money?

If you could have dinner with any famous person who would it be? Would you cook the dinner or eat out? What would be for dinner?

What is your opinion on going to college or working right out of high school?

What is your favorite saying? Who said it? What does it mean to you?

The Story Behind My Adoption:
" One day you'll want to know. I want you to understand"

What was your life like when you got pregnant?

Was it an easy or difficult pregnancy?

What do you (will you) remember most about the pregnancy?

Do you have any regrets about the pregnancy?

How did you feel when you found out you were pregnant?

What do you hope I inherit from your side of the family?

What does my father look like?

What kind of personality does my father have?

How did you first meet my father?

What attracted you to my father?

Where you in a relationship with my father? Are you still?

What can you tell me about my father?

What do you hope I inherit from father's side of the family?

How did you come to the conclusion you would place me in an adoptive family?

What part, if any, was my father involved with decision to place me with a family?

How and why did you choose my adoptive family? Did you have a choice?

Do you feel you made the right decision to place me for adoption? Why?

Who was there when I was born?

Describe to me the day I was born.

Describe to me what it was like for you the first month after I was born,

Do you celebrate mother's day? If so how?

Why would you or would you not want to be in contact with me?

Do you ever think about me?

What do you hope will be different for me then it was for you?

What are your hopes and dreams for me?

What are your fears for me?

Is there anything you wish you could say to me?

Is there anything about you that you want me to know?

Pictures and Mementos:
"A picture can tell a story of a thousand words"

(Please use these few pages to attach pictures, mementos or write any personal notes you would like for your child to have.)

(Please use these few pages to attach pictures, mementos or write any personal notes you would like for your child to have.)

(Please use these few pages to attach pictures, mementos or write any personal notes you would like for your child to have.)

(Please use these few pages to attach pictures, mementos or write any personal notes you would like for your child to have)

(Please use these few pages to attach pictures, mementos or write any personal notes you would like for your child to have.)

(Please use these few pages to attach pictures, mementos or write any personal notes you would like for your child to have.)

Made in the USA
Las Vegas, NV
12 May 2025